Ludwig van Beethoven

FIRST, SECOND AND THIRD SYMPHONIES

in Full Orchestral Score

Dover Publications, Inc., New York

Contents

This Dover edition, first published in 1976, reproduces all the music from the separate volumes of the symphonies edited by Max Unger and published by Ernst Eulenburg, Ltd., London, n.d. (the Editor's Preface to the Second Symphony is dated 1938; to the Third, 1936). In the present volume, the introductions by Wilhelm Altmann (in the Eulenburg volumes these are in their original German with French and English translations) are reproduced in English only—but in a totally new translation—while the three Editor's Prefaces (*Revisionsberichte*), originally in German only, also appear in a specially prepared new English translation.

International Standard Book Number: 0-486-23377-4
Library of Congress Catalog Card Number: 76-10523

Manufactured in the United States of America
Dover Publications, Inc.
180 Varick Street
New York, N.Y. 10014

Symphony No. 1 in C Major, Op. 21

Beethoven had already conceived the plan of a symphony in his early Bonn period. Gustav Nottebohm (*Zweite Beethoveniana*, 1887, p. 567) prints from sketches the opening of a C minor movement labeled "Sinfonia" that corresponds to the beginning of the first Allegro of the Second Piano Quartet, composed in 1785. The same scholar (p. 228) also found sketches for a Symphony in C Major on which Beethoven must have been working in 1794 and early 1795, but never completed. These sketches, which Nottebohm (*Beethoveniana*, 1872, p. 202) at first erroneously connected with the symphony published as No. 1, have no relation to the Symphony in C Major published by Fritz Stein in 1911 from old parts of the Akademisches Konzert in Jena, founded 1780. Whether the latter work is authentic (only the 2nd Violin part is marked "par Louis van Beethoven," and the cello part "Symphonie von Beethoven") cannot be definitely proved, although there are strong claims for its being genuine (cf. Fritz Stein's lengthy discussion in *Sammelbände der Internationalen Musikgesellschaft*, vol. 13, 1911/12, pp. 127 ff.).

It is unclear when the C major symphony published as the First, Op. 21 (for which there are apparently no sketches),[1] was begun; presumably in 1799, since it was first performed at one of Beethoven's own concerts in Vienna on April 2, 1800. On December 15, 1800, and again on January 15, 1801, Beethoven offered it to the conductor Franz Anton Hoffmeister in Leipzig, who, together with the organist Ambrosius Kühnel, had just founded the Bureau de Musique, which became famous very quickly (later C. F. Peters, the well-known firm still in existence today). Hoffmeister & Kühnel published this symphony (of which the original MS is unfortunately lost) in parts at the end of 1801, and this was announced in the *Wiener Zeitung* of January 16, 1802.

The title of this original edition reads: "Grande Simphonie pour 2 Violons, Viole, Violoncelle et Basse, 2 Flûtes, 2 Oboes, 2 Cors, 2 Bassons, 2 Clarinettes, 2 Trompettes et Tymbales, composée et dediée à Son Excellence Monsieur le Baron van Swieten, Commandeur de l'ordre roy. de St. Etienne, Conseiller intime et Bibliothecaire de sa Majesté Imp. et Roy. par Louis van Beethoven. OEuvre XXI. à Leipsic au Bureau de Musique de A. C. Kühnel" (publication number 64).

The first edition of the score was published by N. Simrock in Bonn in 1821 (publication number 1953).

Beethoven did not add the metronome marks until 1817, along with those of Symphonies 2 through 8; all these were published in the supplement to the *Allgemeine musikalische Zeitung*, Leipzig, of December 17, 1817.

Wilhelm Altmann

---

[1] A theme quite similar to that of the Scherzo is already to be found in the hitherto unpublished *12 Deutschen* of 1796/97 (Thayer-Deiters-Riemann, *Beethovens Leben* II, 1910, p. 109).

Editor's Preface to First Symphony

Since the original MS of the work is lost and there is apparently no copy corrected by Beethoven in existence, the basis for the present edition could only be the first edition of the parts or a reprint from the same plates. Such a reprint, obviously, is the copy that was available to me from the archive of the Gesellschaft der Musikfreunde in Vienna, since it differs from the actual first printing only in a slight change in the imprint: "à Vienne, chez Hoffmeister & Comp., à Leipsic, au Bureau de Musique" instead of "à Leipsic au Bureau de Musique de A. C. Kühnel." Examination disclosed that the musical notes themselves show relatively few errors, but that there are numerous inaccuracies in the expression marks, especially the phrasing marks and the ties and slurs. It would be foolish to transfer all such trifling errors to this edition and load down the Editor's Preface with corrections of them. Instead, the attempt has been made to establish the composer's wishes in each case; notes that are obviously wrong have been tacitly corrected, and irregularities in the ties and phrasing have been evened out, if there was no doubt of the composer's intentions.

1st movement, m. 79 (p. 10): The first edition of the parts gives the violas:

The other editions, in order to avoid the parallel octaves and to introduce the third into the chord of the seventh, give:

The passage remains dubious; it is not to be ruled out that Beethoven wanted the version in the first edition of the parts. The present edition adopts the reading of the later publications.

Mm. 95 & 97 (p. 11): In the first edition of the parts, there are staccato dots over the four quarter-notes in the flutes, but slurs over the other winds that are playing quarter-notes. It is clear from the parallel passages near the end of the movement—mm. 248 & 250—that the staccato dots are a mistake and that only slurs can possibly be intended. This incorrect notation, which is not altogether insignificant, has even found its way into the complete edition of Beethoven's works.

Mm. 124 & 125 (p. 15): It is open to question whether the two slurs indicated for the 1st bassoon are not also due to an error in engraving or a slip of the pen on Beethoven's part (compare the 1st violin part, marked for staccato throughout).

2nd movement, mm. 105 & 106 (p. 42): In the first edition of the parts, there is no tie between the two notes c' in the 1st bassoon. Since the effect of it is completely natural-sounding, our edition adopted the usual reading of the later publications, which have the tie.

Mm. 149 & 150 (p. 45): The same situation as the preceding is true of the two horn parts. The two ties have been supplied.

3rd movement, mm. 43 & 44 (p. 52): The first edition of the parts, probably also by mistake, shows no ties in violas and basses. Our edition adopts the reading of the later publications, in which the ties are supplied.

Mm. 133–135 (p. 59): The first edition of the parts gives these unusual expression marks to the two horns:

(with wedge-shaped marks over the notes). This surely must be an error, since most of the other voices have a different phrasing. Therefore our edition follows the later publications, which adapt the horn phrasing to that of the other parts.

4th movement, m. 50 (p. 64): In the first edition of the parts, the first quarter-beat in the 2nd violins reads:

As a comparison with the woodwinds shows, Beethoven surely intended the reading preferred in the later publications:

Zurich

DR. MAX UNGER

Symphony No. 2 in D Major, Op. 36

The D major symphony published as Op. 36 must have approached completion in the village of Heiligenstadt outside Vienna at the time when Beethoven's hearing was already threatened most severely, shortly before he wrote his deeply affecting, melancholy will of October 6, 1802. Sketches for the first movement, occurring in the midst of drafts of the piano and violin sonatas Opp. 23 and 24, the piano sonatas Op. 26 and Op. 27, No. 1, and the ballet *The Creatures of Prometheus*, Op. 43, were published by G. Nottebohm in 1887 (*Zweite Beethoveniana*, pp. 243 ff.). "They do not attain . . . their final form, but on the whole come so close to it that one can conclude that there had been previous work." There are apparently no extant sketches for the Larghetto or the Scherzo. I cannot agree with Thayer-Deiters-Riemann, vol. II, p. 375, and I connect the sketch printed there not with the Trio of the Scherzo of this symphony, but with the Andante of the C minor symphony, as Grove does too, for example. In the so-called Kessler sketchbook, most of which was published by Nottebohm in 1865, there are several drafts of the last movement, the last of which establishes the final version.

The first performance of the symphony, of which the original MS is unfortunately lost, took place on April 5, 1803, in one of Beethoven's own concerts. When the composer's brother Karl referred to a soon-to-be-completed symphony in a letter of March 28, 1802, to the Leipzig music publisher Härtel,[1] when he mentioned a symphony in a letter of November 23, 1802, in reply to an inquiry of the Bonn music publisher N. Simrock; when he once more, on January 22, 1803, offered a grand symphony to Härtel, without results; and when Beethoven himself wrote to Simrock on May 25, 1803: "Then you can also have a grand symphony for only 400 gulden"—all this can only be in regard to the Second Symphony.

The symphony was published in parts by the Vienna Kunst- und Industrie-Kontor, headed by the theater manager Joseph Schreyvogel. The title of this original edition reads: "Grande Sinfonie pour deux Violons, Alto, deux Flûtes, deux Hautbois, deux Clarinettes, deux Bassons, deux Cors, deux Trompettes, Timbales, Violoncelle et Basse. Composée et dediée à son Altesse Monseigneur le Prince Charles de Lichnowsky par Louis van Beethoven. Op. 36. A Vienne au bureau des arts et d'industrie" (publication number 305).

The first edition of the score was published by N. Simrock in Bonn in 1821 (publication number 1959).

Beethoven did not add the metronome marks until 1817, along with those of Symphonies 1 and 3 through 8; all these were published in the supplement to the *Allgemeine musikalische Zeitung*, Leipzig, of December 17, 1817.

Berlin   Wilhelm Altmann

---

[1]Karl von Beethoven's letters to Breitkopf & Härtel were printed by Hugo Riemann in the third appendix to the second edition of vol. II of Thayer-Deiters, *Beethovens Leben*, the printing of which had already been completed. In the first letter he wrote: "Moreover, in three to four weeks we will have a grand symphony and a piano concerto. I request your views about these last two pieces at your convenience, but I would like you to give the first more prompt attention, since we want to see it printed soon, because it is one of my brother's outstanding works." On April 22, 1802, Karl writes: "We would like you to wait a bit longer with the symphony and the concerto, because we still plan to use them in a concert."

Editor's Preface to Second Symphony

Unfortunately the MS of the Second Symphony is lost. In his *Biographical Notes on Ludwig van Beethoven*, Ferdinand Ries states that Beethoven gave it to him but that unfortunately a friend stole it from him "out of pure friendship." Nor has any copy corrected by Beethoven been preserved. Therefore, in preparing this edition I had to rely completely on the first edition of the parts. It is safe to assume, since the work was published in Vienna, that the composer supervised the proofreading. Nevertheless the publication—like almost all the first printings of Beethoven's orchestral works—contains many irregularities, especially unclear slur and tie indications and expression marks. Here, as in all my editing of Beethoven's symphonies and overtures for Eulenburg's miniature score series, it was not my task to present the work exactly as it appears in the first edition of the parts, but to offer a text that would come as close as possible to the composer's artistic intentions. Of course, since there are contradictory indications here and there, it is not always easy to find the right solution. Naturally this is not the place to give all the insignificant differences between the first printing and the present edition. Therefore small inaccuracies, even obvious engraving errors in the notes of the first edition, are not mentioned. Special emphasis is given to errors and inaccuracies in more recent editions, as well as to unclear readings.

First Movement

Mm. 9 & 10 (p. 86): In the first edition of the parts, the 2nd violins have

instead of

This is certainly an engraving error.

Mm. 46 & 47 (p. 92): According to the first edition, the bassoons should play:

Later publications give this reading:

M. 76 (p. 95): It is not quite certain whether or not Beethoven wanted the notes in the horns tied:

In this first of a total of four corresponding passages, the ties are missing in the first printing, but are given once in the recapitulation (m. 248, p. 113). In our edition they are deleted everywhere.

Mm. 77 & 78 (pp. 95 & 96): In the first printing the oboes have

but eight measures later they have

These divergent readings are surely due to an oversight of the composer's. Therefore our edition adopts the reading of the later publications:

M. 134 (p. 101): In the first printing of the parts the

is inadvertently omitted in the first quarter-beat of the 1st flute; this error is to be attributed to the fact that the repeat sign is given after m. 133 rather than after m. 134 (the corresponding repeat sign naturally also occurs *before* m. 34, p. 91).

M. 266 (p. 115): In the first printing of the parts, the violas do not have

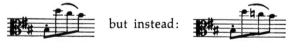   but instead:

This would not be totally inconceivable, but is confirmed neither by the other corresponding voices nor by the exposition (cf. m. 94, p. 97).

M. 346 (p. 123): The first printing of the parts gives the two horns which is perhaps an error of the composer or his copyist attributable to the analogous rhythm in the trumpets and timpani, which enter then. Our edition adopts the reading of the more recent publications:

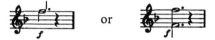

M. 350 (p. 124): The first printing gives the two clarinets a full-measure rest—obviously a mistake; the measure must read

M. 350–352 (p. 124): In the first printing the trumpets have

The usual reading

is preferable, and is adopted in this edition.

Second Movement

M. 32 (p. 127): In the first edition the portato in the 2nd violins and violas begins on the fourth 16th-note. Probably it should start on the second. In general, the first printing leaves much to be desired in the way of consistency and clarity in the matter of indicating portato. In several passages with consecutive 16th-notes of the same pitch, it is a moot point whether portato is desired or not.

M. 56 (p. 129): In the first edition of the parts, the 2nd violins have

A comparison with the similar, but more fully orchestrated, passage seven measures later shows that the sharp sign before the e^1 is an engraving error.

M. 165 (p. 138): Later editions of score and parts omit the 1st bassoon's upbeat

In the first edition the note, which corresponds to m. 8 (p. 126), is preserved.

M. 208 (p. 142): According to the first printing, the horns do not have

as in other editions, but instead:

Third Movement

Mm. 93 & 94 (p. 153): In the first printing, both ¾-notes in all four string parts have small wedge-shaped accents, which call for a pronounced détaché bowing. These important expression marks, lacking in the more recent editions, have been restored in the present text.

Mm. 122–129 (p. 154): Oddly, the first printing gives the 1st bassoon the following three ties:

The later publications show the passage thus, by analogy with the notation of the other instruments:

Can this really have been only an accidental error in the first printing? To be sure, within the full tonal texture this divergent rhythm would not be very noticeable. The usual reading has been retained in the present edition, but the one in the first printing is worth considering.

Fourth Movement

Mm. 52–83 (pp. 159–161): In the first printing, the violas in this *divisi* passage have two staves marked "Viola I" and "Viola II." The same is true of mm. 236–267 (pp. 174–176).

M. 276 (p. 178): In the first edition the 2nd bassoon does not have the single whole note given in the later editions of the score:

 but instead:

Accordingly, it would play along with the cello in this measure only. This notation makes no sense, so the present edition gives the usual reading.

M. 358 (p. 185): In the first printing the 1st flute has

The later editions, including the present one,

have it begin on the first beat of the measure:

that is, in the single and double octave above the oboe and bassoon. A comparison of this dubious passage with the following measures in the woodwinds shows that Beethoven surely intended this reading. In the same measure, the first printing gives the violas

Since the violas also play together with the cellos and basses in the following measures, this reading is certainly another engraving error, and the present edition again adheres to the more

recent publications.

Mm. 426 & 427 (p. 190): The first edition gives the 2nd violins

which was probably another error of the engraver or of the MS he was using. In view of the two preceding measures, the unison with the 1st violins is definitely to be preferred.

M. 438 (p. 192): The first printing gives the two trumpets the octave

Later editions give the unison

The present edition adopts the former reading.

April 1938

Dr. Max Unger

Symphony No. 3 in E-flat Major ("Eroica"), Op. 55

In his 1840 biography of Beethoven (p. 55), Anton Schindler writes: "The first idea for the symphony (heroic, intended for Napoleon Bonaparte) is said to have actually been due to General Bernadotte, who was then French ambassador in Vienna and who esteemed Beethoven highly. I have heard this from several friends of Beethoven. Count Moritz Lichnowsky (brother of Prince Lichnowsky), who was often with Beethoven in the company of Bernadotte . . . , also told me so." On p. 123 of the same book, we read that in 1823 Beethoven still recalled vividly that it was indeed Bernadotte who first inspired him with the idea for the *Sinfonia eroica*. In reality, however, the symphony was not dedicated to Napoleon Bonaparte, although according to Schindler's report, derived from Count Moritz Lichnowsky, at the beginning of the spring of 1804, a fine MS copy of the score had been prepared that was to be sent to Paris through the French embassy in Vienna. In his *Biographische Notizen über Beethoven* (p. 78), Ferdinand Ries reports: "In writing this symphony, Beethoven had Bonaparte in mind, but Bonaparte when he was still First Consul. At that time Beethoven had extraordinary esteem for him. . . . I and several of his closer friends saw a fine MS copy of the score of this symphony lying on his table. At the very top of the title page was the word 'Bonaparte,' at the very bottom 'Luigi van Beethoven,' and not a word more. If and how the space between was to be filled in, I do not know. I was the first to bring him the news that Bonaparte had declared himself emperor, at which he became enraged and exclaimed: 'So he too is no different from an ordinary man! Now he too will trample on all human rights and pander only to his ambition; he will now set himself above all others and become a tyrant!' Beethoven went to the table, grasped the title page at the top, ripped it in two and threw it onto the floor. The first page was rewritten, and it was then that the symphony first received the title *Sinfonia eroica*." This narrative corresponds perfectly with Schindler's report of another eye-witness account, that of Count Moritz Lichnowsky.

The fair copy of the score, written out by a copyist and checked by Beethoven (it was purchased by the Viennese composer Josef Dessauer at the 1827 auction of Beethoven's estate for 3 gulden and 10 kreutzer, and is now preserved in the Archive of the Gesellschaft der Musikfreunde in Vienna, whereas Beethoven's own MS score is lost), was disfigured from start to finish by erasures and corrections. The title page read (partially translated): "NB.1. In the 1st Violin part, the other instruments are partially entered./ Sinfonia grande [here the two words "intitulata Bonaparte" are erased]/ 804 im August/ del Sigr/ Louis van Beethoven/ Sinfonie 3 op. 55/ NB.2. The third horn part is written in such a manner that it can be performed by either a first or second player."

One of the two erased words is said to have been "Bonaparte"; under his own name Beethoven is said to have written in pencil: "Written on Bonaparte."

The date "804 im August" must be a later addition—the darker ink also indicates this—since the symphony was surely completed by 1803, even though Beethoven offered it as a new work to the Leipzig music publishing firm of Breitkopf & Härtel as late as August 26, 1804.[1] The letter says: "The symphony is actually named *Bonaparte*; in addition to the usual instruments there are 3 obbligato horns —I think it will interest the musical public."

The *Eroica* was surely begun by 1801, even though the first movement and the Scherzo date from 1803 (G. Nottebohm, "Ein Skizzenbuch von Beethoven aus d. J. 1803," Leipzig, 1880). Beethoven is said to have been inspired to write the funeral march, with which he was still uncommonly busy in 1803, by the death of Sir Ralph Abercombie, the British general who died of his wounds seven days after the battle

---

[1] On October 14, 1803, Beethoven's brother Karl had already written to that firm about one or two available symphonies, and on November 23, 1803, after the firm had made an offer he considered too low, he had refused it, saying: "You will surely regret this in the future, because these symphonies are either the worst things my brother has written or the best" (Thayer-Deiters-Riemann, II, p. 621). The second of the symphonies mentioned here must have been the just begun C Minor.

near Alexandria on March 21, 1801, but at that time this march was scarcely carried beyond a brief sketch. This occurs in a sketchbook (formerly in the possession of Count Wielhorski in St. Petersburg) that is of great importance for the oratorio *Christ on the Mount of Olives* (completed 1801), and also has material connected with the *Bagatelles* Op. 33 and 119, the piano sonata Op. 31 and the piano and violin sonata Op. 47, but above all contains sketches for the last movement of the *Eroica*. As is well known, this movement consists of variations on a theme that was first composed as a contradance, perhaps even before 1800, and was also used as the finale of the ballet *The Creatures of Prometheus*, completed 1801, and as the theme of the piano variations Op. 35, completed 1802. But even this final movement was thoroughly revised as late as 1803.

Thayer is mistaken in his statements that the *Sinfonia eroica* was first performed before an invited audience one Sunday morning in the Viennese home of the bankers Würth and Fellner (not as early as March 1804), and that a review of it appeared in the *Allgemeine musikalische Zeitung*, vol. 6, p. 467. The first public performance was not until April 7, 1805, in the Theater an der Wien in a benefit concert of Franz Clement, although Beethoven conducted and not Clement.

The negotiations with Breitkopf & Härtel[2] over the publication have been mentioned above. They were quite protracted. On January 16, 1805, Beethoven sent the *Eroica* to Leipzig, but got it back on June 21, since there was no agreement on the payment for it and other works.

The work then was published in parts (announced on October 19, 1806, in the *Wiener Zeitung*) by the Kunst- und Industrie-Kontor (which had already published the Second Symphony) with the title: "Sinfonia Eroica composta per festigiare il Souvenire di un grand' Uomo e dedicata a Sua Altezza Serenissima il Principe di Lobkowitz da Luigi van Beethoven Op. 55. No. III delle Sinfonie. A Vienna nel Contor delli Arti e d'Industria al Hohenmarkt" No. 582 (publication number 512).

Since Beethoven had been blamed for the length of the work,[3] he had the following notice [in Italian] printed on the third page of the 1st Violin part: "This symphony, which is longer than usual, should be performed closer to the beginning than to the end of a concert, and shortly after an overture, an aria and a concerto, so that it may not be heard too late, when the listener is already tired by the earlier works and may lose the special desired effect."

The first score edition was published by N. Simrock in Bonn in 1821 (publication number 1973). Beethoven had had his brother Karl write to Breitkopf & Härtel on February 12, 1805: "My brother also thinks it would be profitable to you to print this symphony in score in a small format, like those of Haydn in Paris, since all connoisseurs would surely make it their business to acquire it."

Beethoven did not add the metronome marks till later, at the same time as those for Symphonies 1, 2 and 4 through 8; all these were published in the supplement to the *Allgemeine musikalische Zeitung*, Leipzig, of December 17, 1817.

WILHELM ALTMANN

---

[2] Cf. Oskar v. Hase, *Breitkopf & Härtel; Gedenkschrift*, 4th ed., vol. I, 1917, pp. 168 ff.

[3] "My brother thought at first, before he had heard the symphony, that it would be too long if the first part of the first movement were repeated, but after it was performed several times, it proved actually prejudicial not to repeat the first part": letter from Karl van Beethoven to Breitkopf & Härtel, February 12, 1805.

Editor's Preface to Third Symphony

In preparing the present edition I was able to consult the copy of the MS corrected by Beethoven that is in the collection of the Gesellschaft der Musikfreunde in Vienna, and the first printing of the parts, a mint copy of which is in the large Beethoven collection of Mr. H. C. Bodmer in Zurich. I am also greatly indebted to several most helpful persons for oral or written information: Dr. Hedwig Kraus, who subsequently checked various passages in the above-mentioned MS copy, Mrs. Carmen von Weingartner-Studer, Mr. Antony van Hoboken and Prof. Hans Gál, all in Vienna. In addition, I made use of the second part of Heinrich Schenker's essay "Beethoven's Third Symphony" in the third volume of his yearbook *Das Meisterwerk in der Musik*, Munich, 1930. (As meritorious as that study is in many respects, it still does not exhaust the topic by far.)

Since Beethoven's autograph MS of the *Eroica* is lost and both the copy he corrected and the first printing of the parts contain many obvious inaccuracies, a restoration of the original form of the music is impossible, and even if the original MS existed, it would probably turn out that an edition that reproduced it exactly would be hardly desirable. Not to mention outright errors in the notes—not a rarity with Beethoven—his autograph scores, especially, generally contain many inaccuracies in indicating dynamics, slurs and ties and other aspects of phrasing. Nevertheless it is the highest duty of an editor of musical masterpieces to be as faithful as possible to the composer's intentions, and thus to correct his oversights and slips of the pen. Because of the shortcomings of the sources, this is not always easy, especially in a new edition of the *Eroica*.

For reasons of space I cannot enumerate the many small differences between the present edition and the above-mentioned MS copy and first edition of the parts. That would become an essay as long as Schenker's. But several dubious passages and undoubted improvements, some of them not mentioned by Schenker, must be discussed here.

1st movement, mm. 150 & 151 (p. 207): In his essay "Notes on the Correct Performance of Beethoven's Symphonies" in the *Neue Wiener*

Musikzeitung of 1853, Beethoven's pupil Carl Czerny made the following important remarks about this passage: "I still possess the instrumental parts of the *Eroica* in the original edition, which was published by the then existing Kunst- und Industrie-Comptoir about 1805 under Beethoven's supervision. According to this, the end of the first part [of the first movement] is as follows:

The two measures here marked with asterisks were omitted in Simrock's score, destroying the rhythm of the whole passage. Thus [on page 18 of that score] a *bis* should be added for all the parts over the last two measures on that page." Beethoven scholarship had completely overlooked that direction of Czerny's until I went into the matter in Max Hesse's *Deutscher Musikerkalender* for 1914. Unfortunately I was not yet familiar with the first edition of the instrumental parts, so I could only repeat Czerny's indication and trust that it was right. In an essay published shortly afterward in the journal *Die Musik*, Theodor Müller-Reuter attacked the statement by Beethoven's pupil and my paper, and referred to a later edition of the engraved parts preserved in the archive of the Gesellschaft der Musikfreunde in Vienna. That edition still shows clearly that the four measures in question were changed into two. In all the appropriate voices the original notes were scraped away and replaced by the shorter version, but because of the inexpert workmanship the old version can still be recognized fairly clearly. Recently I was able to examine the parts edition with the Kunst- und Industrie-Kontor imprint that is preserved in Zurich, and made the same observation that Müller-Reuter had made with the later impression. In another edition, owned by Antony van Hoboken in Vienna and said to be a first printing, the original four measures have already been changed to two. This is in contradiction to Czerny's statement that in his copy the two measures in question were repeated. There are two different approaches to resolving the discrepancy: either the passage was already altered while the first printing was in progress, or else the copies now in the Zurich Beethoven collection and in the possession of Antony van Hoboken in Vienna are both part of a later edition of the work by the Industrie-Kontor. In the MS copy corrected by Beethoven, which to be sure does not seem to have been the engraving copy, the two measures are not repeated but are themselves crossed out and then restored to validity by the word "gilt" [all right; stet] repeated several times. But who countermanded the original repetition in the first edition? If it was Beethoven himself, Czerny would of course be wrong. Without a doubt, however, once one has grown used to the repetition of the measures, one will agree with Beethoven's disciple that they are perfectly metrical. (By the term "unrhythmical" Czerny means "unmetrical.") Unfortunately the question cannot be finally decided, and it must be left to the judgment of the conductor whether the first or the abridged second reading should be used. It should also be observed that in his arrangement of the symphony for two pianos, which was published long after the composer's death, Czerny naturally also upheld the repetition of the two dubious measures.

Mm. 543 & 544 (p. 239): In the MS copy corrected by Beethoven, as well as in the first printing of the parts, the 1st and 2nd violins have

but in the later editions:

that is, the two clearly indicated flat signs at the asterisks have been turned into natural signs. It is arguable whether this is correct, since the two flat signs are confirmed four times in the above-mentioned sources, which must remain the most important indicators for all new editions. Nevertheless it is open to question whether the composer intended the passage that way, since not even in the old sources does the parallel passage at the end of the exposition (m. 141, p. 206), in the key of the dominant, B-flat, concur with the version given first above.

Mm. 657 & 658 (p. 251): In the MS copy corrected by Beethoven and the first printing of the parts, the trumpets have

but conductors incorrectly have them play

on the false assumption that the trumpet did not yet normally play a g^2 (cf. p. 89 of Schenker's essay). It should be emphasized that both in the MS copy and in the first-edition parts the second of the two measures does not show the division into eighth-notes

given in the later editions, but has sustained
¾-notes

Since the trumpets, in contrast to most of the other winds and brasses, do not have sub-divisions into eighth-notes even before this measure, it is still by no means certain that the composer did not really intend the sustained notes in this measure, as in the last music example. In the present edition the later, usual, reading has been adopted, but the passage is still subject to the opinion of the conductor.

2nd movement, mm. 51 & 52 (p. 261): In the MS copy and first-edition parts, the 2nd violins have

but in the usual publications:

Since I cannot see why the fifth of the chord should be lacking in this passage, I have restored the earlier version in the present edition.

Mm. 230 & 231 (p. 290): In the first edition of the parts, the 2nd horn has but in the MS copy corrected by the composer, as well as in the later editions:

Since all the other winds have an eighth-note and an eighth-rest, the lithographer of the first edition probably thought that the quarter-note in the 2nd horn was an error in the MS. Naturally, the usual reading is correct.

3rd movement, last two measures on p. 306: In the MS copy corrected by Beethoven and in all editions, including the first printing of the parts, the two oboes have

It is perfectly clear from the immediately following measures (top of p. 304) that the former reading is a mistake in instrumentation on the part of the composer. In the editions up to the present, the last notes more or less hang in the air. (I am grateful to Prof. Hans Gál in Vienna for pointing out this error.)

M. 316 (p. 309): According to the usual editions, the oboes play

but according to the MS copy and the first-edition parts, they play

which is certainly correct.

Mm. 355–371 (pp. 310–312): In the first-edition parts the horns have

But there is an entry on the MS, seemingly not in Beethoven's handwriting:

This is the reading adopted by the later editions. In the present text the earlier version has been restored, but the passage remains dubious, since the other version may be based on Beethoven's own wishes.

4th movement, m. 20 (p. 321): As the conductor Carmen Studer-Weingartner assumes, perhaps correctly, the indication "arco" is missing here in the strings. There are various points in support of this opinion: the change in note values from the preceding pizzicato passage; the staccato dots that the first edition of the parts shows for the string bass line on the four eighth-notes of m. 26; the new pizzicato indication in m. 31; and, not least, the fine effect achieved in the passage by this manner of performance. Of course, an unanswerable proof is not forthcoming, and the execution of the passage must be left to the judgment of the conductor.

Mm. 350 & 351 (p. 347): The MS copy and the first printing give the clarinets

whereas the later editions interchange the two voices as follows:

The present edition restores the earlier reading, which is certainly correct. (On this, cf. also p. 92 of Schenker's above-mentioned essay.)

Zurich   July 1936

Dr. Max Unger

Symphony No.1

I

L. van Beethoven, Op. 21
1770 – 1827

2

Allegro con brio (♩ = 112)

7

8

9

10

18

28

32

II

Andante cantabile con moto (♪=120)

36

38

41

42

44

III

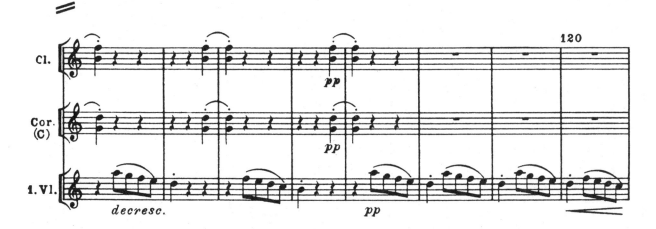

58

Menuetto da Capo
(Pag. 50)

60

IV.

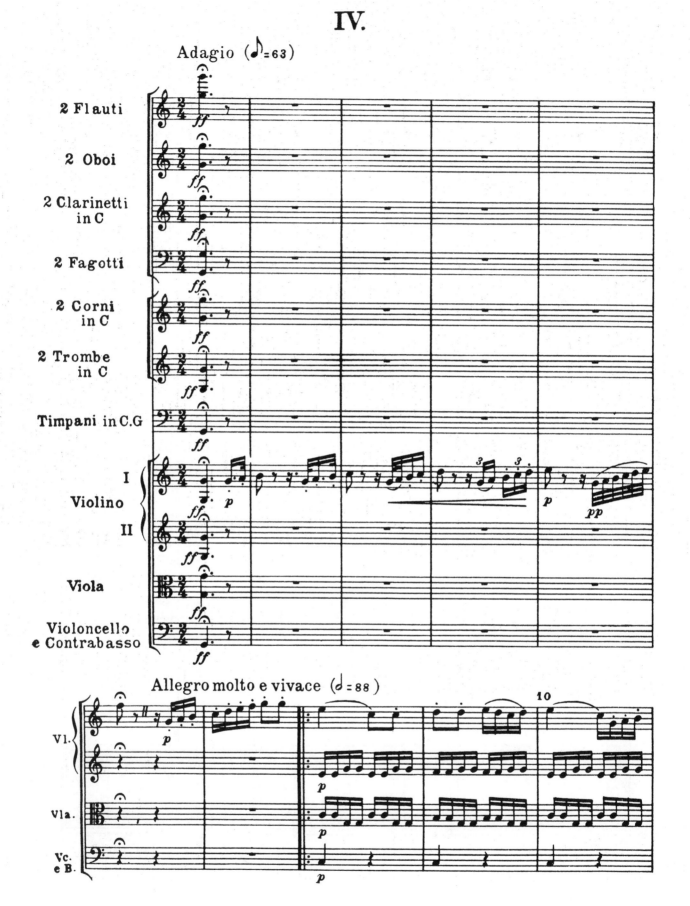

62

64

66

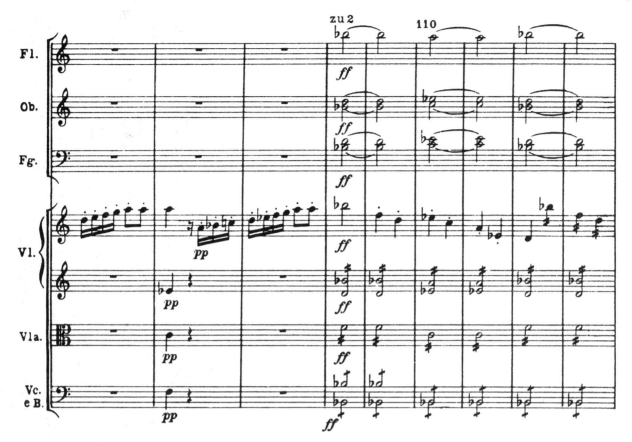

71

72

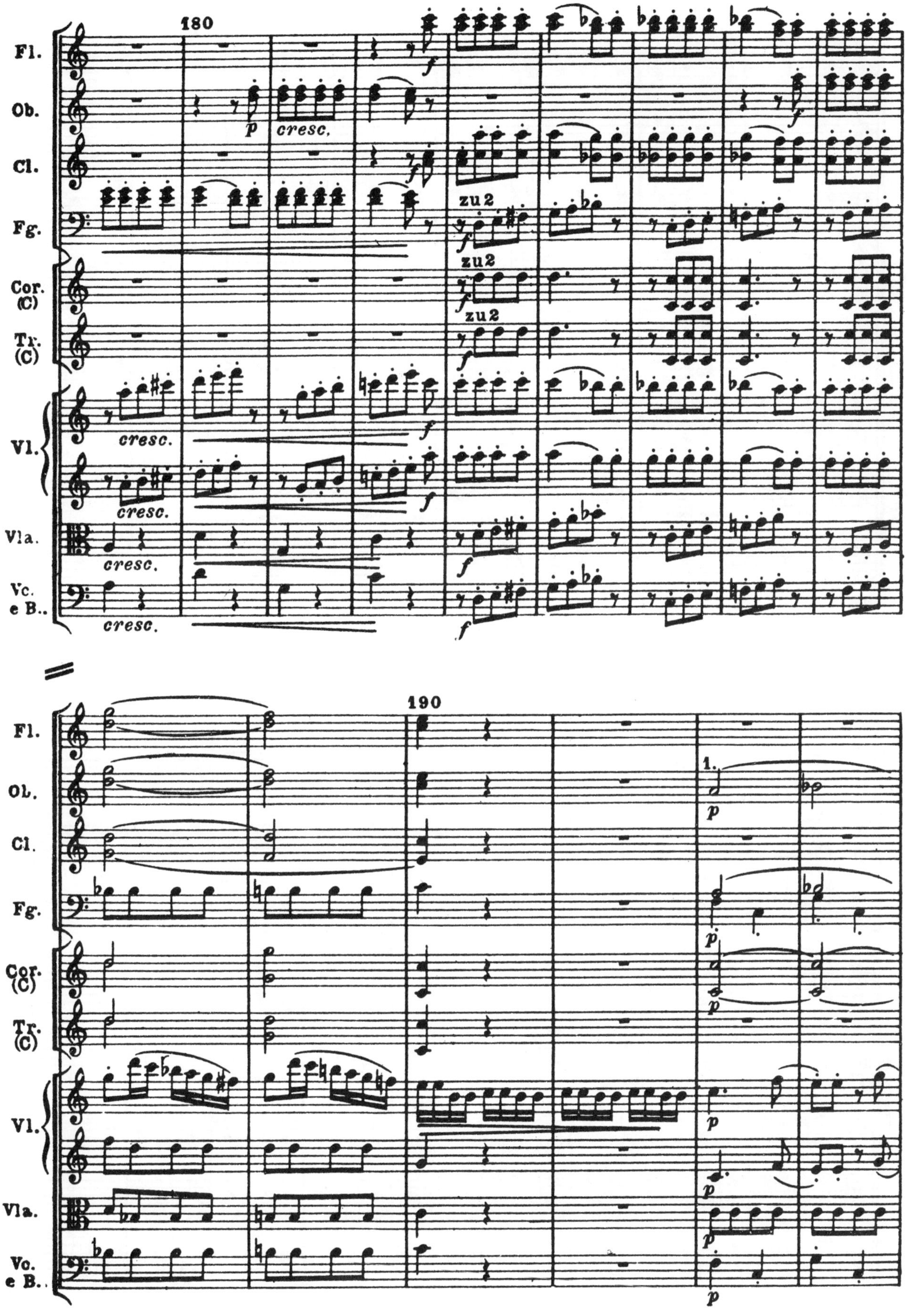
180
Fl.
Ob.
Cl.
Fg.
Cor. (C)
Tr. (C)
Vl.
Vla.
Vc. e B..
cresc.
zu 2
190
1.
p
f

76

82

Symphony No. 2

I.

Adagio molto (♪ = 84) L. van Beethoven, Op. 36
1770-1827

87

90

Allegro con brio ($\mathtt{d} = 100$)

94

108

110

115

116

270

120

II.

Larghetto ($\flat$ = 92)

127

128

130

132

138

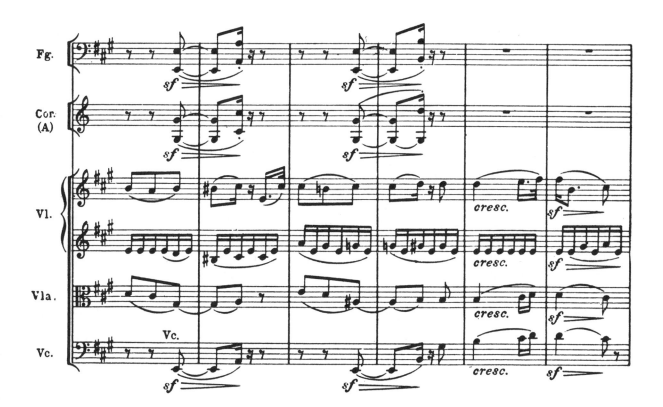

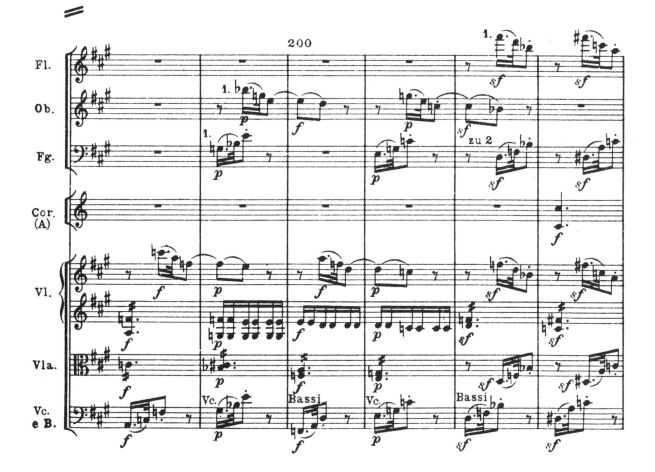

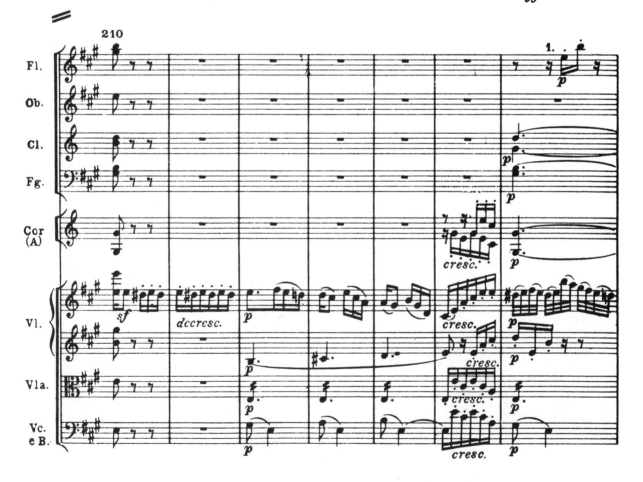

III.

Scherzo Allegro ($\dot{\,}$. = 100)

151

152

154

Scherzo da Capo

IV.

Allegro molto

($\downarrow$ = 152)

156

167

230

178

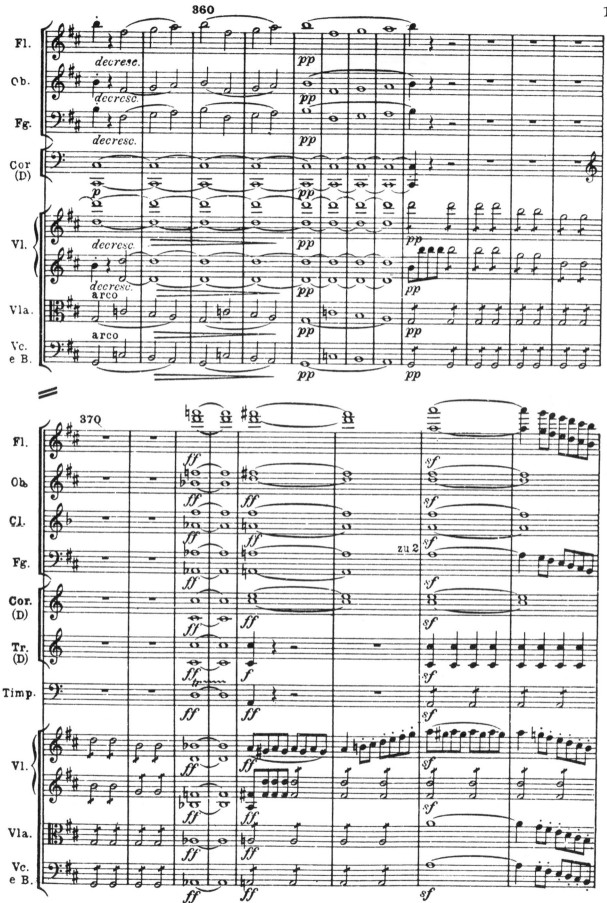

188

Symphony No 3

I

Allegro con brio ♩.=60

L.van Beethoven, Op.55
1770-1827

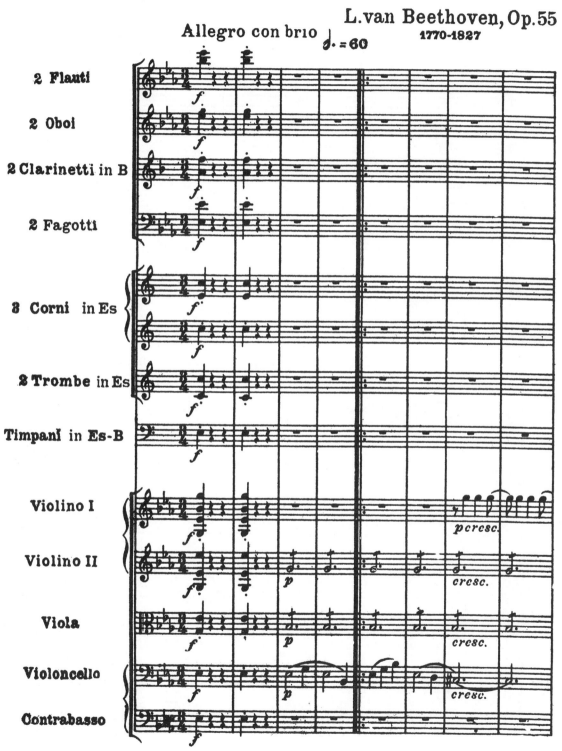

196

200

205

208

209

212

216

218

223

224

225

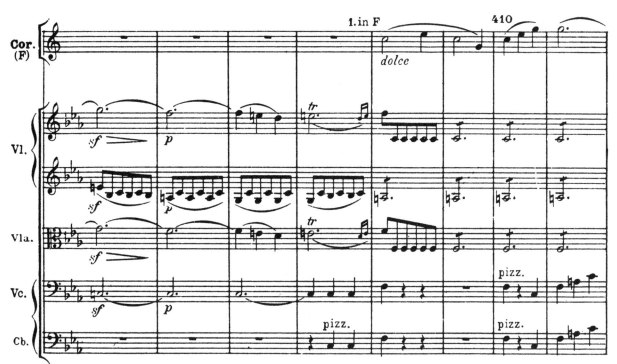

226

236

244

252

255

256

II
Marcia funebre. Adagio assai ♪=80

264

268

274

150

275

283

290

280

291

III

Scherzo. Allegro vivace ♩.= 116

296

Trio

310

312

Coda

IV

Finale Allegro molto

332

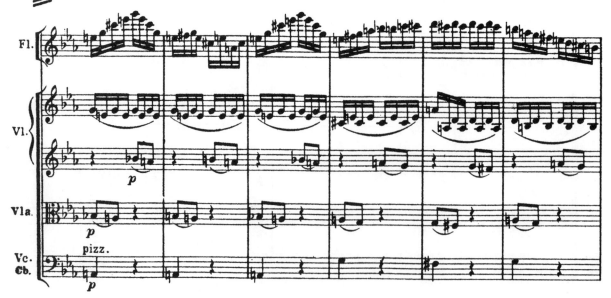

340

350

351

354

364